Little Yogi's BIG FEELINGS

JANESSA GAZMEN

"A beautiful and insightful book that connects BIG feelings with action. A great tool for children (and grown ups) to build self-awareness and emotional intelligence."
—Dr. Rumeet Billan, PhD, learning architect, humanitarian and author of *Who Do I Want To Become?*

"*Little Yogis Big Feelings* asks important questions in a heartfelt and inviting way, while providing playful and actionable strategies to nurture emotional balance and wellness..."
—Jill Hewlett, Brain Fitness Expert & Wellness Authority, author of *Common Sense...Uncommonly Practised.*

"...a must-have for mindful parents...Here's to a future of emotionally intelligent children!"
—Paul Galloro, Mindful Movement Educator and Creator of ARISE.

Dedicated in loving memory to my Mother, who has shared in all my joys, sorrows, trials, and achievements; and whose love has been my anchor. Her passion for this project as in all my endeavors was never less than my own.

I love you, Mom.

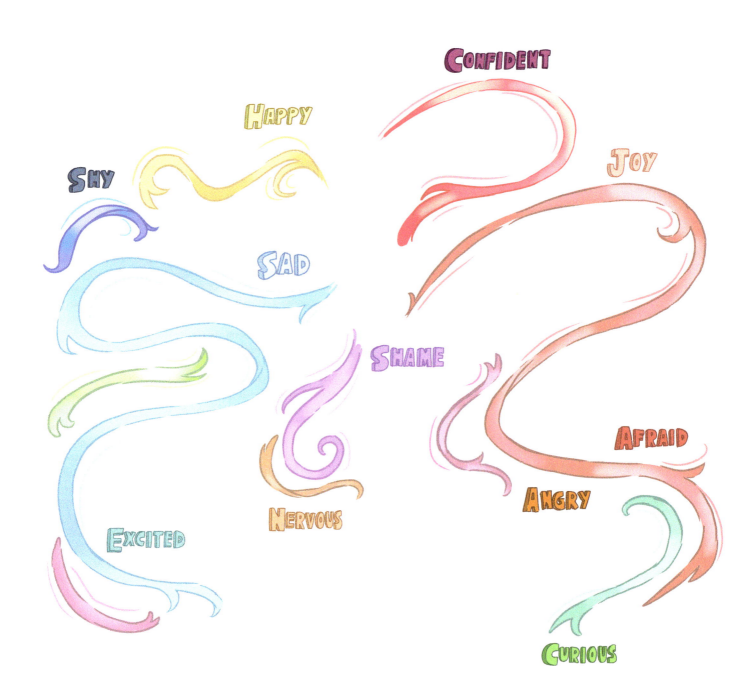

Introduction

Helping kids learn to become aware, to label and to manage their emotions will cultivate skills that can help them cope during challenging situations. Skills like resilience, self-awareness, focus, connection, and empathy will be strengthened. Giving kids the opportunity to choose their own practice each day lets them know that they have emotional rights. This not only empowers them and gives them control, but it also helps them maintain healthy boundaries. Once the reader pinpoints their feelings, they will be directed to the page which corresponds to their self-identified emotion. Each feeling will offer breathing techniques, yoga poses, a yogi promise, and a journaling opportunity to help the reader manage their emotions.

Are you a little yogi with big feelings?

A yogi is anyone who does yoga. If you've never done yoga before, you'll become a yogi today!

Everyone, even little yogis, have big feelings. Feelings come from emotions. To figure out your emotion, listen closely to your body and to what it's telling you. It's important to become quiet and to focus so you can listen carefully and often, since feelings can change many times.

Sometimes emotions can make you feel good, and sometimes they can make you feel sad. It's ok for little yogis to face all of these big feelings. Just remember that little yogis are always the boss of their feelings. You can express emotions that spread laughter, and you can calm emotions that make it seem like a rainy day.

The fun exercises in this book will help little yogis express feelings like joy and happiness. They will also help them deal with hard feelings like sadness and anger.

Breathing can help calm little yogis so they can deal with big feelings.

Yoga which involves breathing and exercise can give little yogis energy, make them stronger, and even help get rid of the grouchies.

The **Yogi Promise** will remind little yogis that they are the boss of their own big feelings and will help little yogis make healthy connections with loved ones.

The **Journaling Exercise** will help little yogis use their imagination and unleash the creativity that every little yogi has.

1. What are you feeling, little yogi? Knowing how you feel can help you talk about it. It's time to get quiet and listen to your body. Ask these questions to help discover your feelings.

When I wake up after **Sleeping**, do I have energy to meet the day *or* am I still tired?

Am I **Breathing** fast *or* slow?

Is my **Heartbeat** loud *or* soft?

Is my **Tummy** feeling good *or* uneasy?

What else do I notice in my **Body**?

2. After you discover what your body is telling you, use the list on the next page to find your big feeling exercises.

3. When you find your big feeling exercises
- Breathe
- Do yoga poses
- Repeat the little yogi promise
- Listen to your body and then journal about your big feeling.

CHOOSE YOUR BIG FEELING

Happy

Go to page 12

Joy

Go to page 14

Excited

Go to page 16

Confident

Go to page 18

Curious

Go to page 20

Nervous
Go to page 22

Shame
Go to page 26

Shy
Go to page 24

Sad
Go to page 28

Angry
Go to page 32

Afraid
Go to page 30

It's fun to pretend we're **animals** to help **express big feelings.**

YOUR BIG FEELING IS
HAPPY

Because of their friendly face, dolphins always look like they're smiling. But really, they express emotions by clicking and whistling. Pretend you're a dolphin and breathe in from your blowhole at the top of your head while whistling or clicking. Bring both hands over your head. Breathe out and move your hands down like water spouting out from your blowhole. Repeat 10 times.

TODAY IS GOING TO BE a GREAT DAY I CAN SPREAD HAPPINESS to others

Repeat this yogi promise 5 times.

Write about your BIG FEELING

Listen to your body.

Rising Tide

Stand tall. Breathe in, sweep your arms up and reach as high as you can. Look up to the sky.

Flipper Dive

Breathe out, bend down, and dive your arms to the ground. Let your head and arms hang.

Dolphin Leap

Standing tall, bend your knees and step one foot all the way back behind you. Lift both arms towards the sky. Take 3 breaths, then switch legs.

YOUR BIG FEELING IS
JOY

Pandas love to tumble and play. They bring joy wherever they go. To save energy, Pandas breathe slowly, taking only 6-10 breaths every minute! Little yogis breathe much faster, taking up to 20 breaths per minute. Get your panda bear breath on. Breathe in while counting to 4 and trace each finger on your panda paw from bottom to tip. When you reach the tip, hold your breath for 4 counts. Trace your finger back down and breathe out while counting to 4. Repeat this breath with each finger on both hands.

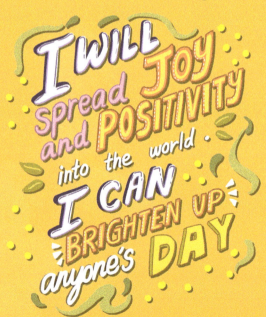

Repeat this yogi promise 5 times.

Write about your BIG FEELING

Listen to your body.

Bamboo Stalk

Breathe in, sweep your arms up and look up to the sky when you stretch.

Panda Walk

Bend your knees and walk your hands forward on the ground. Straighten your legs and raise your tail up. Take 3 breaths, then walk your hands back and stand tall.

Bear Chair

Bend your knees and imagine you're about to sit on a chair. Hold your tail in the air and stretch your arms forward as far as you can. Take 3 breaths, then stand tall.

YOUR BIG FEELING IS
EXCITED

Rabbits breathe mostly through their noses, not their mouths. It helps them eat while they breathe. Rabbits also breathe much faster than little yogis do. Do the bunny breath. Sit on your knees, make bunny paws in front of you. Take 4 quick sniffs in like a bunny. Let out a long, slow breath. Repeat 10 times.

Repeat this yogi promise 5 times.

Write about your BIG FEELING

Listen to your body.

Carrot Dig

Kneel on the floor, sit back on your heels. Rest your forehead on the floor and stretch your hands out in front. Take 3 breaths.

Rabbit Tail

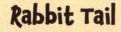

Stand on your hands and knees. Lift your knees and tail off the ground, then straighten your legs. Relax your head and neck and look through your hind legs. Take 3 breaths.

Bunny Hop

Jump your feet forward wide towards the outside edges of your hands. Then stand up.

YOUR BIG FEELING IS
CONFIDENT

Not only are giraffes the tallest land animals, but they can communicate without making any sound! Only at night can you hear them hum. Breathe quietly like a giraffe. Sit cross-legged and reach both arms towards the sky. Hold your palms together and breathe in while reaching tall. Take 10 breaths.

I am Helpful and can set a GOOD EXAMPLE FOR MY FRIENDS and FAMILY I CAN DO ANYTHING I PUT MY MIND TO

Repeat this yogi promise 5 times.

Write about your BIG FEELING

Listen to your body.

Tall Giraffe

Bring both hands up with your palms together. Reach left and hold while taking 3 breaths. Then reach right and take 3 breaths.

Thirsty Giraffe

Standing with your feet wide apart, bend forward at the hips and bring your hands to the ground. Take 3 breaths, then stand up.

Picking Leaves

Kneel on the floor. Stretch one leg out to the side with your toes pointing up. Reach one hand to the sky with the other hand resting gently on your leg. Take 3 breaths. Then switch sides.

YOUR BIG FEELING IS
CURIOUS

Monkeys are curious, smart, and eager to learn. Did you know that they can even count? Pretend you're a monkey and count your breaths. Sit cross-legged with your hands in your lap. Breathe in 1. Breathe out 2. Breathe and count to 20.

I AM EXCITED TO LEARN NEW THINGS TODAY
I AM SMART
I CAN LEARN QUICKLY.
I PRACTICE THINGS to grow my skills

Repeat this yogi promise 5 times.

Write about your BIG FEELING

Listen to your body.

Banana Squat

Step both feet wide apart. Bend your knees and squat like a monkey while placing your right hand on the floor to the outside of your right foot. Stretch your left arm to the sky and look up. Take 3 "oohoohaahaah" breaths. Then switch sides.

Tree Swing

Step one foot back, bend your front knee, stretch your arms towards the sky, and look up. Take 3 breaths. Repeat this with the other foot behind.

Jungle Tree

Stand on one leg. Bend your lifted knee and place the bottom of that foot on your standing leg. Balance and hold. Take 3 breaths. Repeat on the other side.

YOUR BIG FEELING IS
NERVOUS

Horses get nervous for many reasons like when they are separated from their family or when they are bored. You can tell they are nervous when they tremble or run away. Let's breathe like a horse. Sit cross-legged. Breathe in through your nose while counting to 4. Hold your breath for 4 seconds. Breathe out through your mouth while flapping your lips like a horse. Repeat 10 times

Being NERVOUS is UNCOMFORTABLE but I CAN HANDLE IT

I AM LOVED even if I make MISTAKES

Repeat this yogi promise 5 times.

Write about your BIG FEELING

Listen to your body.

Tickling Butterflies

Lie on your back, bend your knees, and bring the bottoms of your feet together. Press your hands together and rub your palms until they feel warm. Place your warm hands on your belly. Take 3 breaths.

Horseshoe Scrub

Lie on your back with your knees bent, pointing up to the sky and with your feet flat on the ground. Tuck in your chin and lift your bum off the ground. Straighten one leg and lift your foot up. Hold for 3 breaths, then bring your foot back down. Repeat on the other side.

Horseback Rider

Stand tall with your feet apart, bend your knees, and pretend to sit down on an imaginary horse saddle. Hold for 5 breaths.

YOUR BIG FEELING IS
SHy

Deer are shy and timid; they don't like much attention. Deer also love to eat dandelions. Sit cross-legged with hands on your lap and palms facing up. Imagine you're a deer smelling a dandelion and breathe in. Then blow all the dandelion seeds away through your mouth. Repeat 10 times.

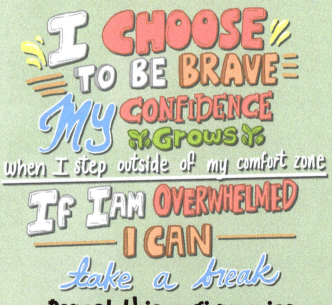

I CHOOSE TO BE BRAVE
MY CONFIDENCE Grows
when I step outside of my comfort zone
If I am OVERWHELMED I CAN take a break

Repeat this yogi promise 5 times.

Write about your BIG FEELING

Listen to your body.

Tail Swish

With your hands and knees on the floor, breathe in and lift your right arm off the ground, straight in front of you. Lift and stretch your left leg out behind you. Take 3 breaths, then repeat on the other side.

Graceful Deer

Stand tall with your arms alongside your body. Lift and bend one leg behind you. Use your hand to hold your ankle or foot up. Breathe in and stretch the other arm in front of you. Balance and take 3 breaths. Repeat on the other side.

Leaping Deer

Step one foot behind you and step your other foot in front. Bend your front knee and straighten your back leg while lifting your arms like a 'T.' Hold for 3 breaths. Lift your back leg in the air and lean forward. Take 3 breaths. Repeat on the other side.

YOUR BIG FEELING IS
SHAME

It's easy for turtles to hide. They just tuck into their protective shells. Turtles can even hold their breath underwater for hours to hide from danger. Pretend you're a turtle. Sit cross-legged with your hands on your lap. Take a big breath in through your nose and squeeze your shoulders up towards your ears. Hold your breath for 4 counts. Breathe out of your nose for 4 counts and relax your shoulders back down. Repeat 10 times.

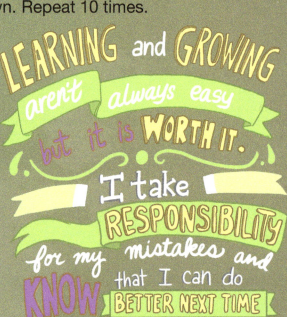

LEARNING and GROWING aren't always easy but it is WORTH IT. I take RESPONSIBILITY for my mistakes and KNOW that I can do BETTER NEXT TIME

Repeat this yogi promise 5 times.

Write about your BIG FEELING

Listen to your body.

Hiding Turtle

Sit on the ground and stretch your legs wide with your knees slightly bent. Then, bend forward and slide your arms under your legs. Hold for 3 breaths.

Ocean Swim

Lie on your belly, reach your arms straight in front of you, and rest your forehead on the ground. Then lift your head, arms, chest, and legs away from the ground. Stretch and take 3 breaths, then lower back down to the ground.

Beached Turtle

Lie on your back with your arms and legs relaxed. Take 3 breaths.

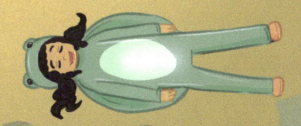

YOUR BIG FEELING IS
SAD

Bumblebees are gentle. They will only sting if they feel scared, sad or hurt. You can tell a bumblebee is close if you hear a buzzing sound. Buzz like a bumblebee. Breathe in and smell your flower. Breathe out with your mouth closed and make an MMM-sound like a humming bee. Repeat 10 times.

I've defeated CHALLENGES BEFORE and I CAN DO IT AGAIN. Letting others know HOW I FEEL is taking care of my EMOTIONS.

Repeat this yogi promise 5 times.

Write about your BIG FEELING

Listen to your body.

Busy Wings

Bend your elbows and keep hands together. Bring your elbows up, circle backwards 3 times, circle forward 3 times, then flap your elbows up and down like wings.

Beehive

Step your feet wide and raise your arms like a 'T.' Bend over your front foot and reach down. Stretch your upper arm to the sky. Hold for 3 breaths. Repeat on the other side.

Flower Power

Sit tall and bend your knees with the bottoms of your feet together. Weave your arms underneath your legs. Lift your chest and hold your legs up. Take 3 breaths.

YOUR BIG FEELING IS
AFRAID

Elephants are gentle giants who can be afraid of anything that moves quickly and suddenly. Did you know that elephants can eat up to 300 kilograms of food every day? That's 200 times more than what little yogis eat! Do some elephant belly breaths. Lie on your back with your hands on your belly. Breathe in through your nose for 4 counts and fill your whole belly with air. Feel your belly expanding. Hold for 4 counts. Exhale and let all the air out for 4 counts. Feel your belly relax. Repeat 10 times.

I am surrounded by people who love and support me. I am safe. I can tell my fear to leave and let go of my worries. This might be hard but I can handle it.

Write about your BIG FEELING

Repeat this yogi promise 5 times.

Listen to your body.

Swinging Trunk

Bend forward with your arms hanging down. Bring your palms together and link your fingers. Sway side to side while you're bent forward. Then stretch your trunk high into the sky. Breathe out and make a big trumpet sounds.

Floppy Ears

Step your feet apart and bring your hands to the top of your head. Move your elbows front to back, like elephant ears.

Grazing Trunk

Step one foot behind and bend the opposite knee. Stretch your arms like a 'T.' Then bend back while lowering your back arm down toward your back leg. Bring your front arm up to the sky. Hold for 3 breaths. Repeat on the other side.

YOUR BIG FEELING IS
ANGRY

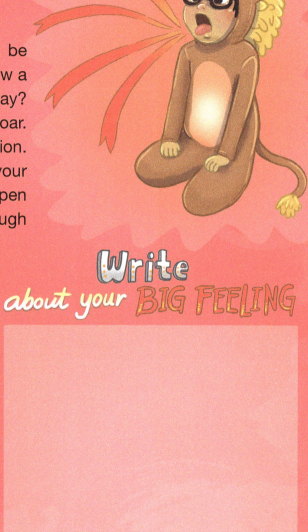

Lions are the King of the Jungle. They can be aggressive and scare other animals. Did you know a lion's roar can be heard from miles and miles away? Imagine you're a powerful lion and get ready to roar. Sit on your knees and lean on your heels like a lion. Breathe in. Open your mouth wide, stick out your tongue, and stretch it down towards your chin. Open your eyes as big as you can and breathe out through your mouth with a loud RAWR! Repeat 10 times.

I am the KING of my own feelings ...AND... **I can control my own BEHAVIOUR**. **I choose KINDNESS** because it feels good. **I can be kind** even when it is hard. **I can take quiet TIME** when I need it.

Repeat this yogi promise 5 times.

Write about your BIG FEELING

Listen to your body.

Lion Pounce

With your knees and elbows on the floor, link your fingers together. Lift your knees up and press your tail high. Take 3 breaths and rest your knees back to the ground.

Rip Roar

Lie on your belly and place your hands on the floor. Begin to straighten your arms and lift your chest off the floor. Breathe in and with a loud RAWR, breathe out. Lower down to the floor.

Resting Lion

On your hands and knees, sit back on your heels. Reach your arms out in front of you and rest your hands on the ground. Spread your knees wide apart and place your forehead on the floor between your knees. Take 3 breaths.

One Printers Way
Altona, MB R0G 0B0
Canada

www.friesenpress.com

Copyright © 2023 by Janessa Gazmen
First Edition — 2023

All rights reserved.

No part of this publication may be reproduced in any form, or by any means, electronic or mechanical, including photocopying, recording, or any information browsing, storage, or retrieval system, without permission in writing from FriesenPress.

ISBN
978-1-03-913369-3 (Hardcover)
978-1-03-913368-6 (Paperback)
978-1-03-913370-9 (eBook)

1. JUVENILE NONFICTION, SOCIAL TOPICS, EMOTIONS & FEELINGS

Distributed to the trade by The Ingram Book Company

About the Author

Janessa Gazmen is a certified yoga teacher (e-RYT) and member of the Yoga Alliance. She has been teaching both family yoga and kids yoga since 2012. Having taught all ages from four-year-olds to ninety-nine-year-olds, Janessa has seen first-hand how connected our body, minds, and spirits are. She is passionate about bringing the peace and strength of that connection to children all around the world.

Janessa lives in Markham, Ontario, Canada, with her husband Robbie; their two children Sienna and Noah; and their puppy Moshi.

CPSIA information can be obtained
at www.ICGtesting.com
Printed in the USA
BVHW010315310123
656817BV00001B/1